# Another, An Other Photography

by Ira Schneider

Ira Schneider asks you to look at the world through his eyes, just for a bit.

Ira is one of the media art world's necessary people. People like this turn up at the appropriate time and change everything forever. Often, they don't just do one thing. Unlike many artists, who bend their heads over their work and seldom look up and are valuable people in themselves, these others are multi-talented, with a vision that can entirely encompass their discipline. They make contributions with their art, but also with their minds, and always, they hope, for the benefit of all. They struggle with the future. They make a difference, as Americans like to say.

Ira is one of these. He stands out as an editor of video literature, being a founder and co-editor of *Radical Software*, and co-editor, with Beryl Korot, of the book, *Video Art, an Anthology*, 1976 that necessary snap shot of what video art was back in 1975, a crucial period.

He is one of the two artists (the other being Frank Gillette, another necessary man) who created *Wipe Cycle*, 1969, a handsome and successful time delay video piece that totally inaugurated the use of arrays in video art, and then went on to produce a number of multi-channel works. He was a principal member of Raindance, an important early video collective, a media think tank that spawned not only *Radical Software* and the book Guerrilla Television, but also, in a later manifestation, a whole new way of doing television journalism.

He is also an aphorist, a channel to Karl Kraus, enjoining us to enjoy depression while it lasts. [Schneider's e-book *Enjoying Drepression* is available at the iTunes store.]*

Sometime back in the 70s, when Andy Grundberg was writing in the Sunday art section of the New York Times, there was a moment in video art when some artists posed the notion that one of the many streams leading into video art was photography. It could also lead out, or partway out in some cases. Frank Gillette, Peter Campus, and William Wegman among others, added photography to their oeuvre, and in the case of Campus, pursued it entirely for some years. Photography did offer something that was hard to get from video, even though video offered movement and sound. It offered better resolution and better color and gray scale. More important, though, photography offered a contemplative moment. Video was always a time-based art, even at its most still. Photography invited you to think about a certain 50th of a second.

Photography was a messy business back in those days, very removed from the operational simplicity of half-inch video. Clicking the shutter was only the beginning; what followed was a detailed process involving further optics, chemical baths, temperature control, all carried out in a darkish room with water running, relieved only by a dim red light. Hours could be spent.

Photography today is almost nothing like that except for the participation of the lens, the light, and the eye. But we don't even call it digital photography anymore, it's just photography, the way it is now. Everything is instant. Cell phone cameras are ubiquitous, they have been for some years now. For those that want them, they make big digital cameras, looking not unlike the old SLRs, with changeable lenses and an array of manipulative options. They also do video. Good video. Some people doing video favour these cameras.

How would you quantify a comparison with the number of photographs taken today with numbers from back in the mid seventies? No can do. But it has to be fair to say that there is an enormous amount of photographic activity in the world, and that it encompasses people, and peoples, who were mostly absent back in the chemical era. It's probably fair to say that some of this output, even most, has only a digital life, seldom seeing paper. Still, much of the content would be familiar to dark room denizens of the past; family pictures, friendship pictures, sentimental objects, pets, communications between lovers. And there are work photos, on the job note-taking, aides memoirs. What was that long registration number? Taking a picture of it is easier than writing it down. And there is social journalism; people at riots, demonstrations and war zones, and people just on the street, making photographs and transmitting them, pressing a button and sending them off somewhere. And all of this is instantaneous and going on all the time. It is another of the great 21st century changes.

Ira has a lifetime of examined visual experience behind him; photography is not new to him, he's labored in the darkroom in the 1950s and 1970s. But he has fully accepted the revolution (well, he'd better) and is now ***Driven to Abstraction***. The title conjures interesting interpretations. One is the sense that he's done everything else (he actually has mostly) and abstraction is a last resort. There could be others; perhaps a car was involved. Consider also the possibility that it is this new paradigm of photography that has driven Ira to abstraction, or if not that, exactly, to recording in detail images selected from the activity of his eye. From vision to resolution in an instant.

The process itself lends itself to immediacy, rare in photography of the past. Abstraction and immediacy are not often thought of together. But those are the bookends that we have to consider when looking at Ira's photographs. Ira can take a hundred pictures a day and more if he wants to. We are used to thinking of immediacy as involving human interaction, but there is immediacy here as well. When looking at Ira's photographs one can see all the others like it that he discarded. The there are 57 images in ***Driven to Abstraction*** but the impression is of thousands.

Not that the offerings in ***Driven to Abstraction*** are abstract in the usual sense; they can be viewed (some of them) that way if we squint a little or look at them from a certain distance. But we are looking at them closely here. And what we have are mostly identifiable objects seen in extreme closeups, accumulations involving lots of plastic bags, some scenes that are reminiscent of museum installations of the seventies (I'm thinking of a coil of plastic conduit here). There is also one featuring a man, situated in what looks like a grotto, surrounded by a tiny aircraft, the Blessed Virgin Mary, an azure shield with a dog argent on a leash proper, and the disembodied head of someone, could be a young Lenin, but it might be his assistant.

There is one other with humans in them, a medal and chain bedecked, young woman reaches out to a figure on the run; to catch her, to point her out? It is a cartoon without a caption. The expression is magnetic, one is drawn to it.

But like Ira's accumulations of plastic bags it is the accumulation of photos, one after the other that arrests. The soul of ***Driven to Abstraction*** is not in the individual photographs, though they are poignant, but in the stream of photographs that photography today encourages. It carries photography on the way to becoming a time based medium. Nan Goldin famously did a 45-minute slide show of 800 slides. That's 3.75 seconds per photo. [Less known is Ira's series "2000+12, 2000+13 & 2000+14" where in each year: 2012, 2013 & 2014 he projects 2000 images (two at a time - 67 minutes) and hangs either 12, 13 or 14 depending on the year.]*

For other artists the accumulation of photos is significant in other ways. Artist Nancy Cain works like this. She photographs houses, cars, signs, birds, sunsets, people sometimes, anything she likes at the moment. Individual photos do stand out, she follows her mind's focus, and she publishes every day to a list of admirers. From the photographs of Nancy Cain, one could probably recreate the entire town of Desert Hot Springs, her main subject.

[Schneider's ***Configurations*** chapter extends this concept of accumulation. Some of his configuration series are composed of as many as 30 related images.]*

***Driven to Abstraction*** is a good moment in photography, one that epitomises a whole new paradigm and carries it to length. Ira is not young, but he is always new.

Also, Ira does very little that is not in some way funny. That could be from any distance; his humour is both microscopic and telescopic, he sees the big funny and the little funny, and those in between. So we are challenged to see the humour in all of this. Believe me, it is there.

D.G.

Davidson Gigliotti and Ira Schneider met in 1969, the infant year of independent video, D.G. with the Video Freex and I.S. with Global Village & later Raindance. They worked together in 2002 to put the early video magazine, *Radical Software* on the internet. They are planning now to make, the 1976 published, Video Art an Anthology available on the internet.

* Editor's supplemantary statement

# Driven to Abstraction

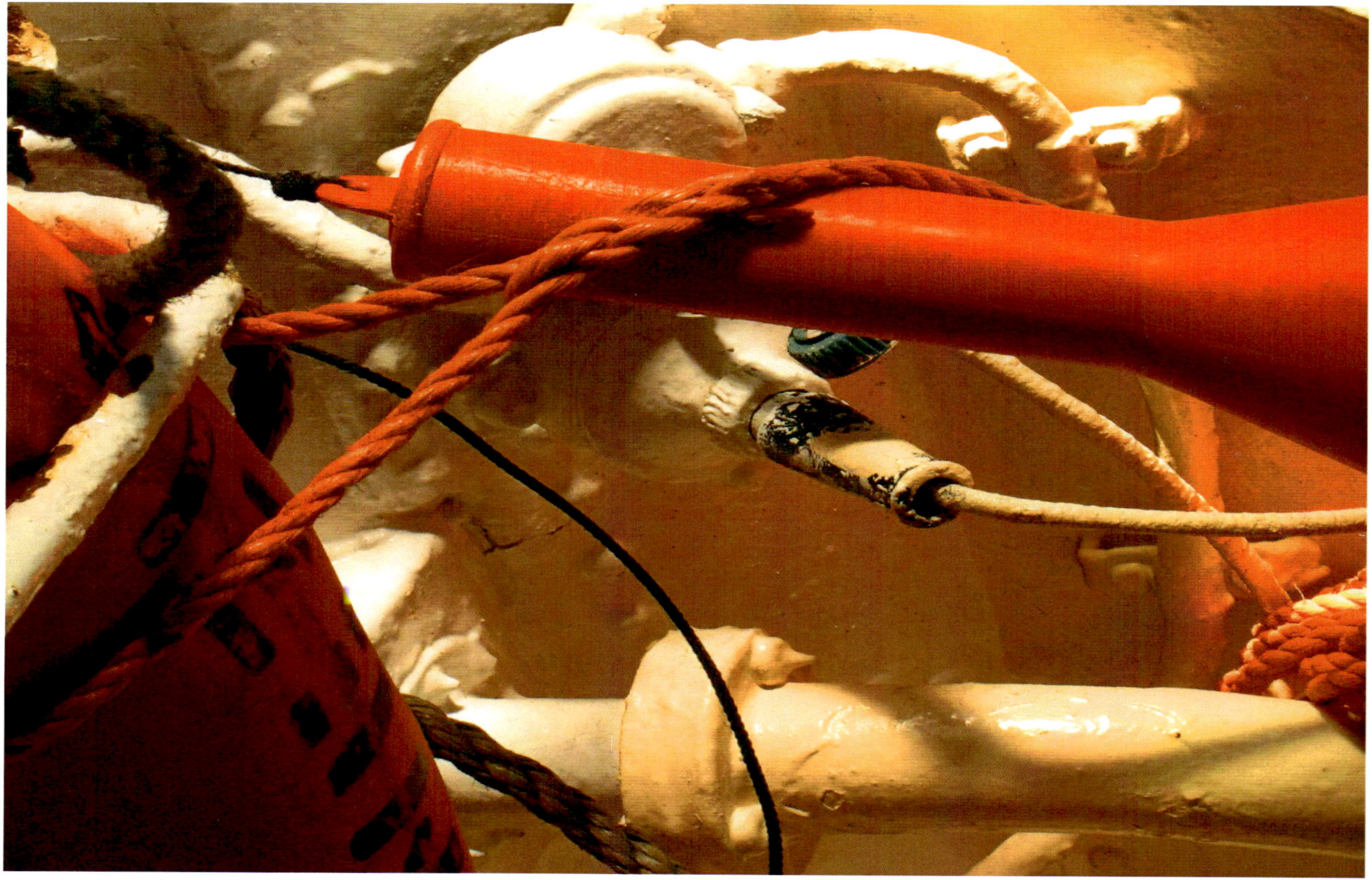

BURGER KING

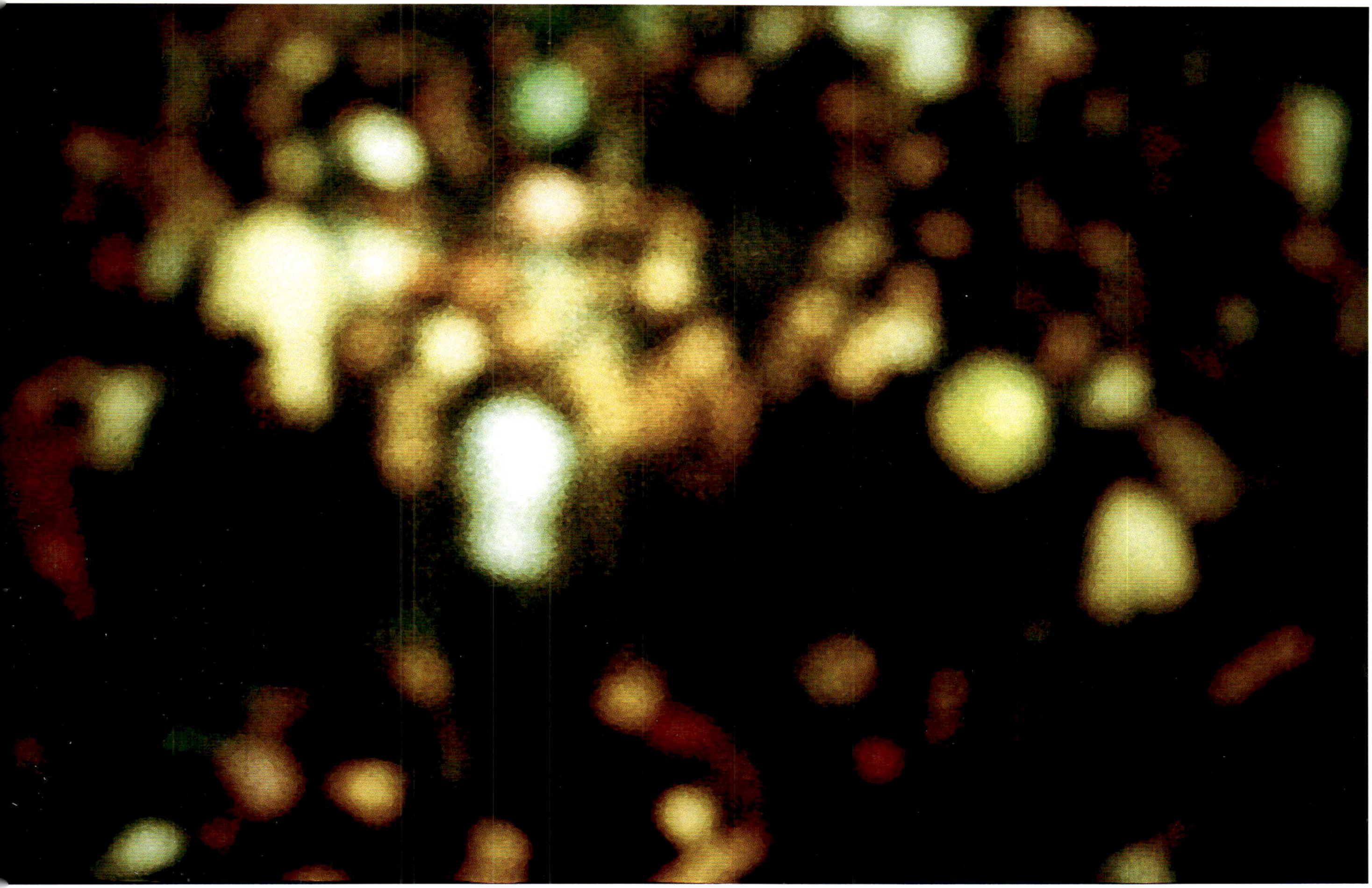

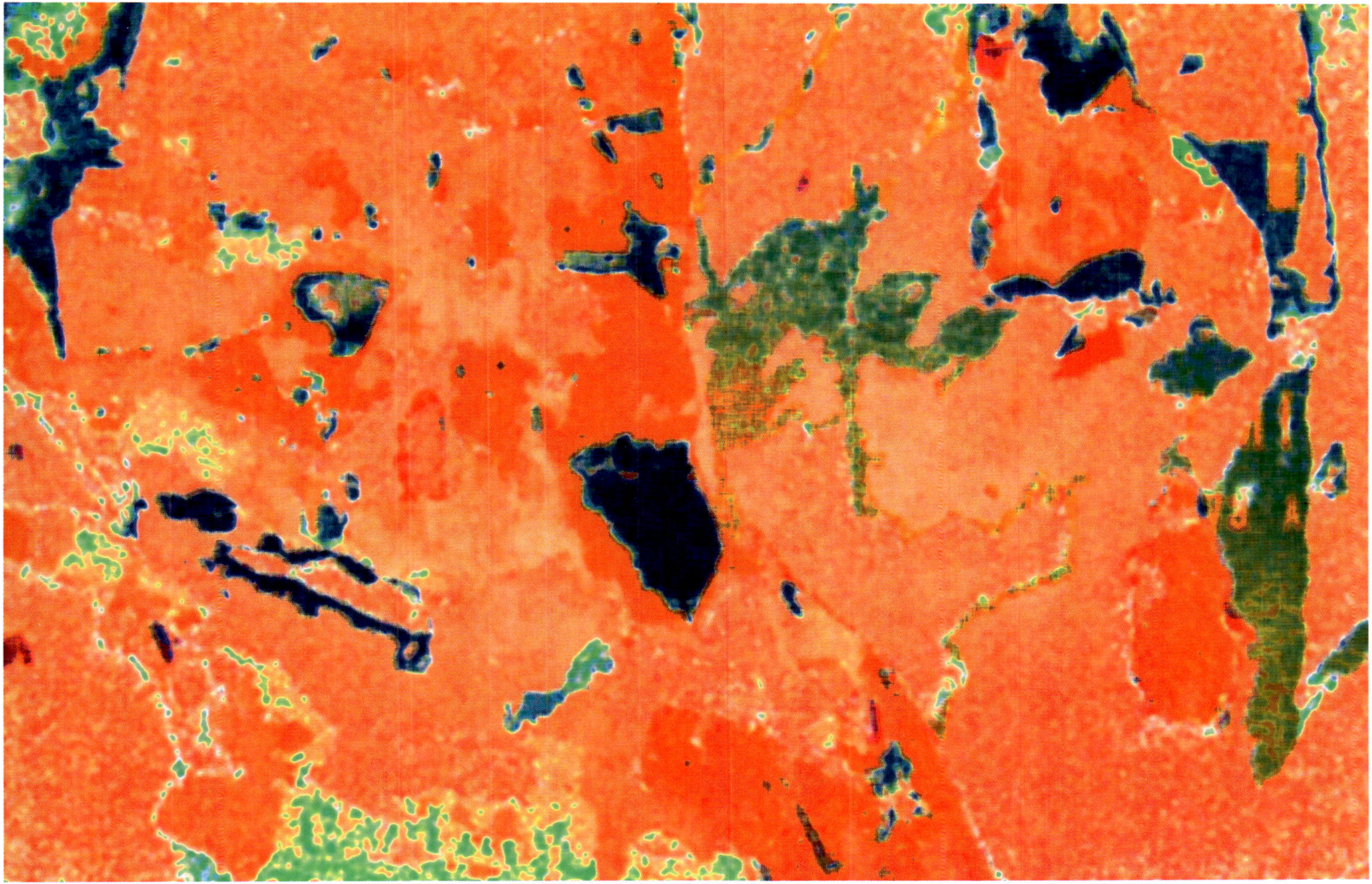

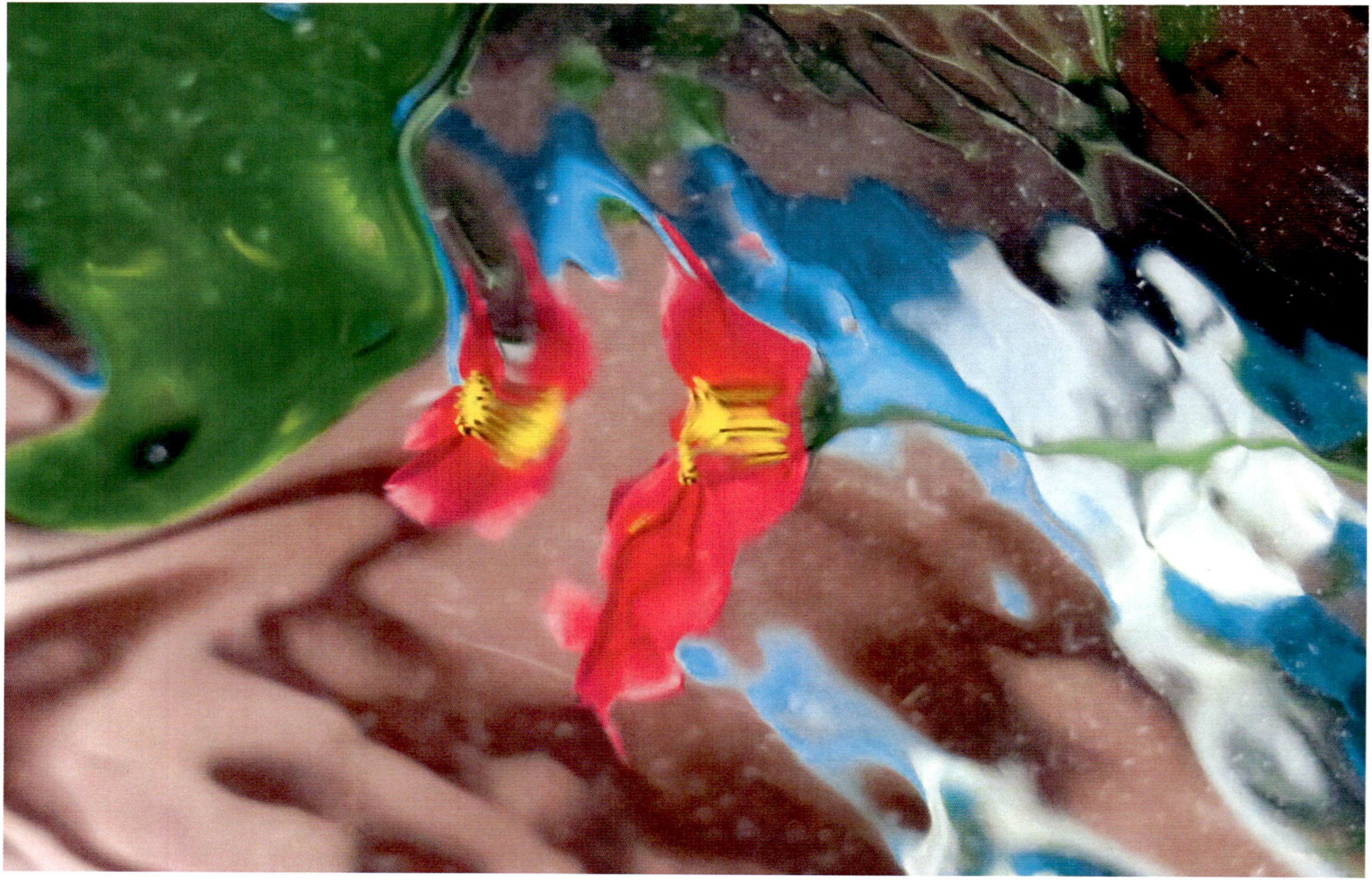

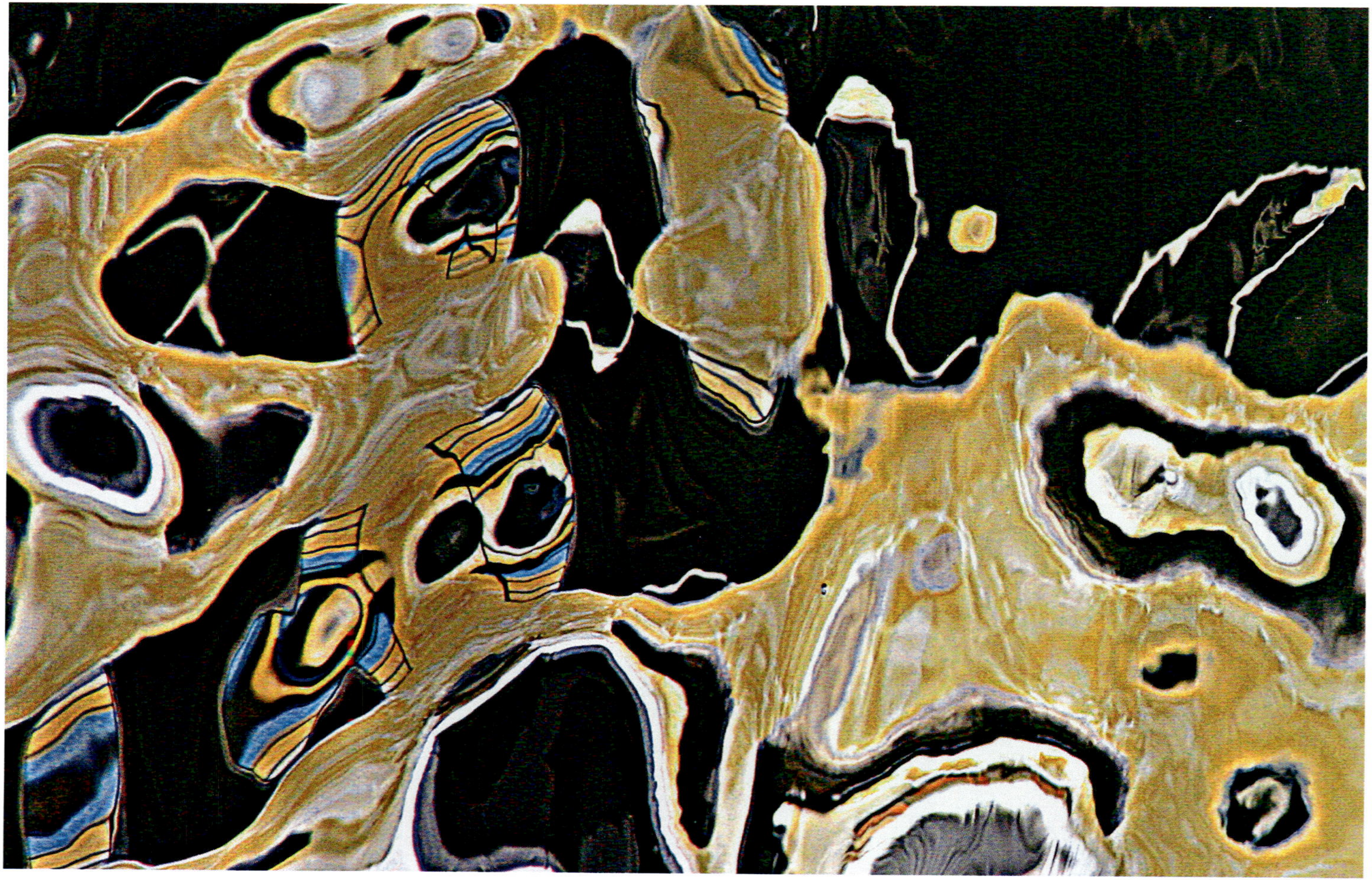

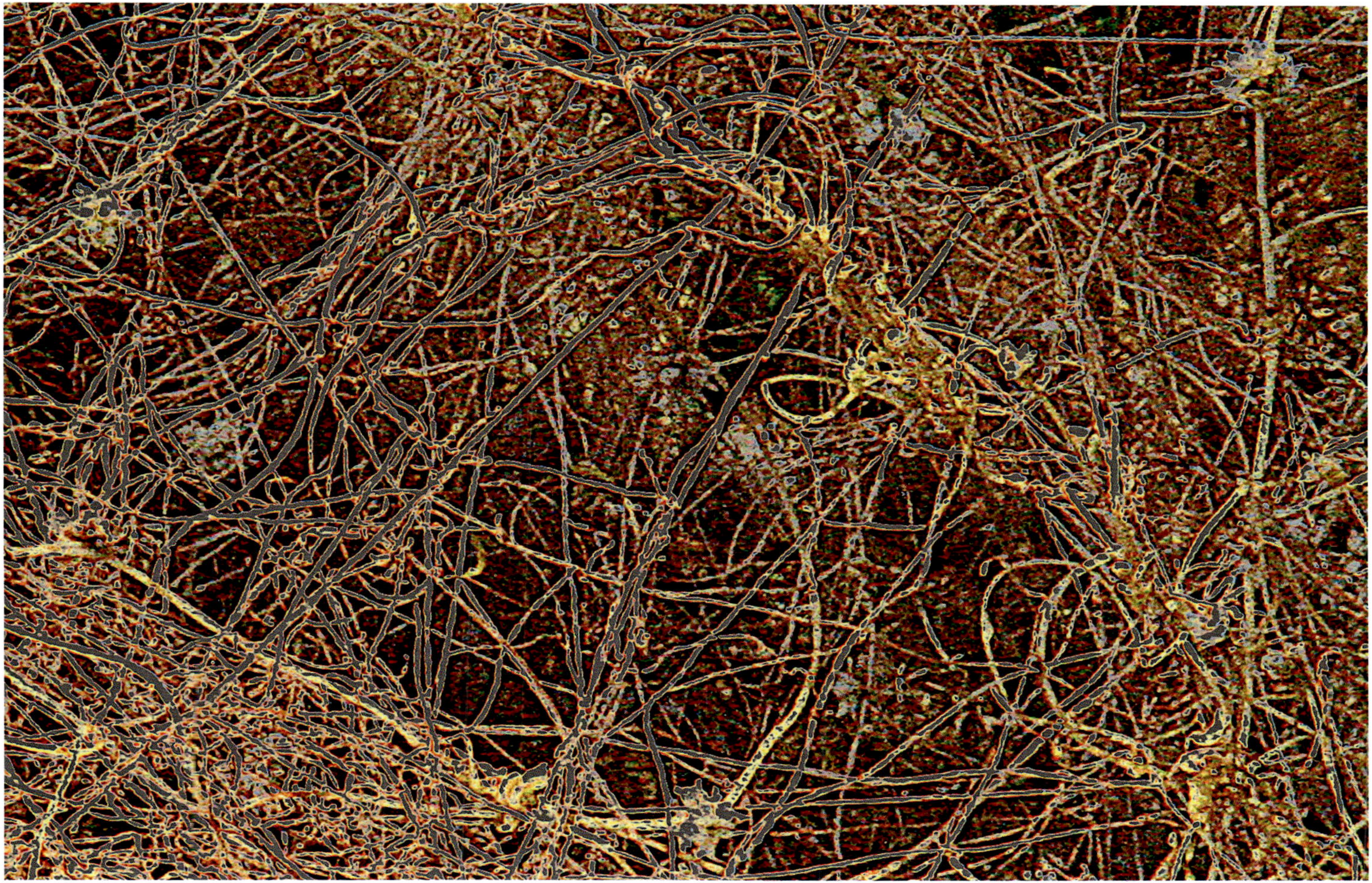

# Configurations

KATZEN

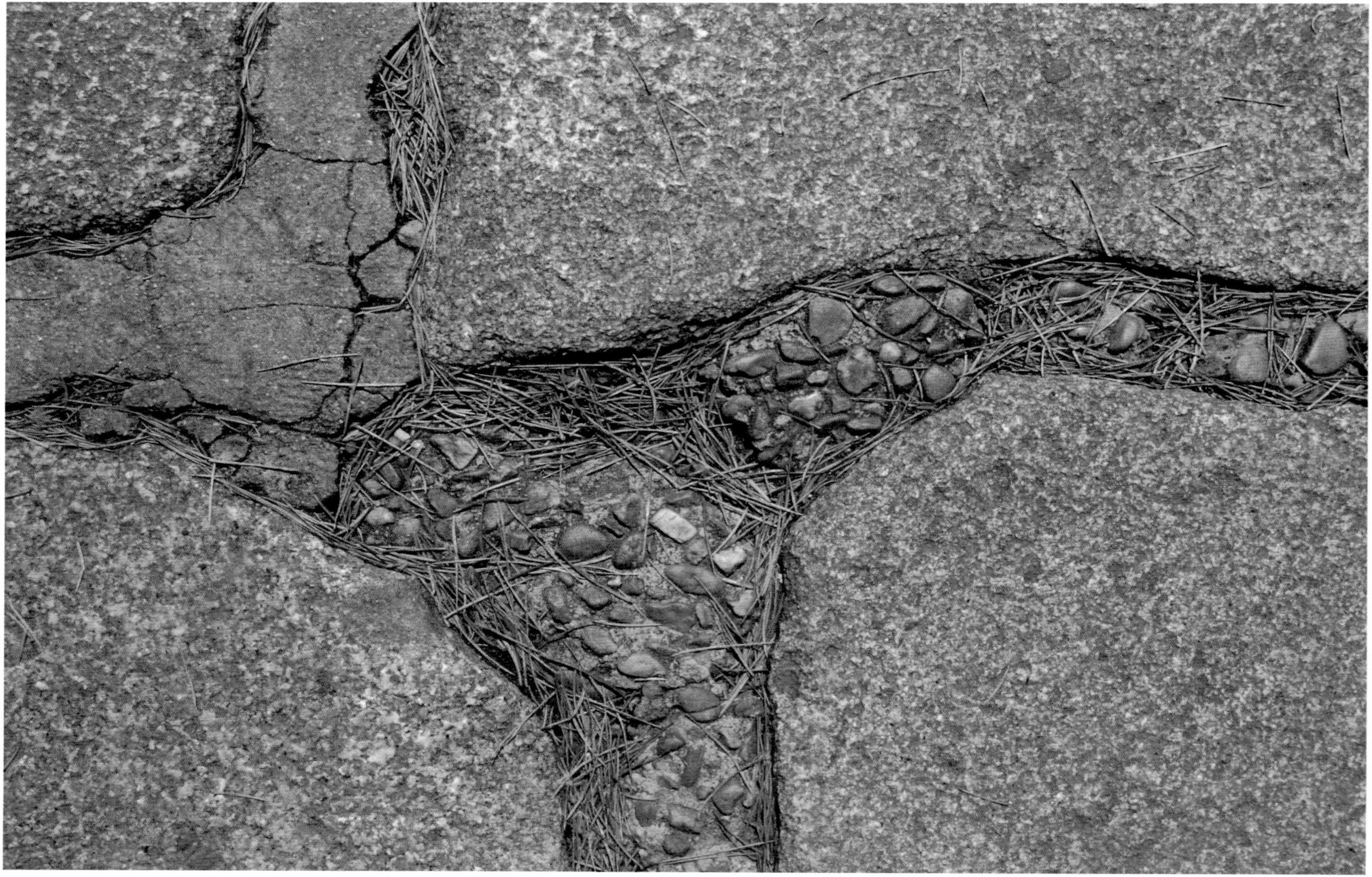

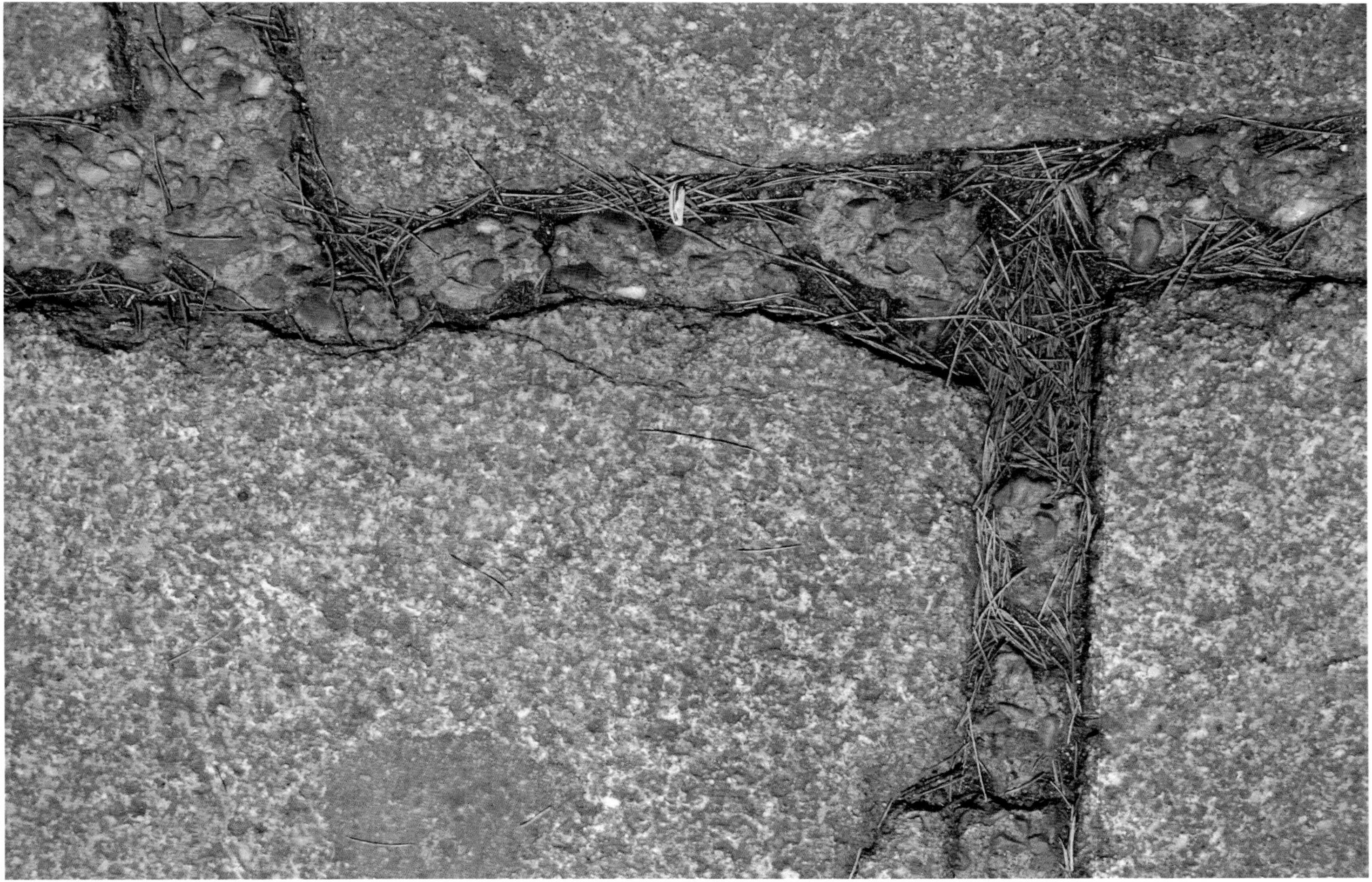

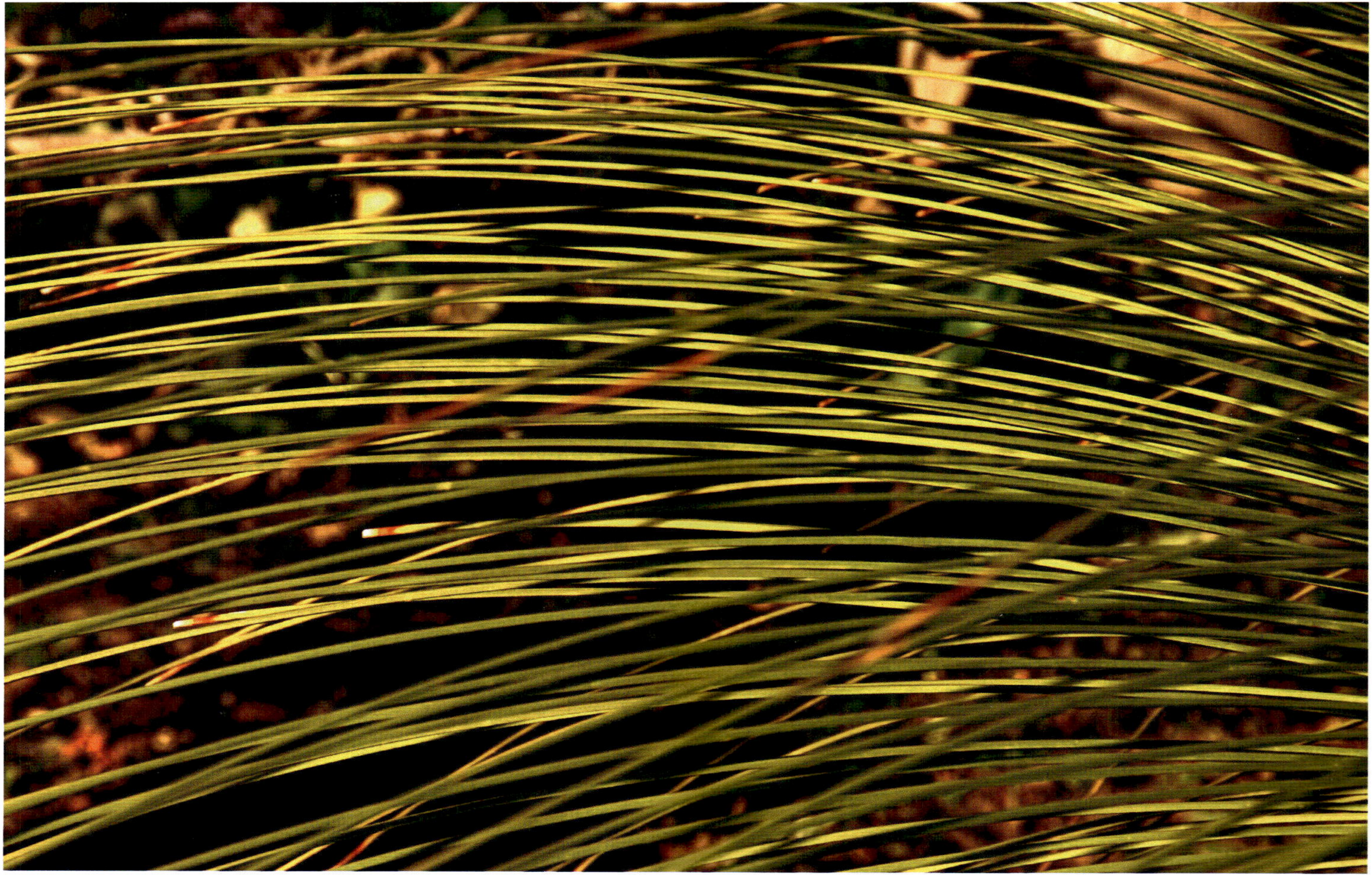

Ira Schneider is one of the great abstract humorists of our time as well as a documentarian of wide resources. In his work, these two fields of activity do not compete but rather merge into a single, often surreal experience which can peer below the surface of things to plumb the act of perception itself. If it is up to the rest of us to parse the meaning thereof, then the act of viewing his photos becomes a radical act in and of itself, a kind of descent into the possibilities of physical properties.

As Protagoras said, man is the measure of all things, and Schneider's work recalibrates both the physical and metaphysical facts of life – perhaps the Washington Monument is really only five foot eight. While the facts on the ground remain firmly on the ground, they are no longer required to be facts and indeed, the ground itself is likely to shift, revealing a sprawling colorfield that can be quite beautiful, even dramatic at times. His photos capture the miracle of motion through the stasis of light; they can be poetry, a request for directions, or, indeed, a recipe for a delicious quiche. To Schneider, these elements all merge nicely into a single reality: the photo image.

While his images are specific to time and place they are not required to bare resemblance to either or to what passes for the facts as they arrive through our perceptive filters; colors and shapes take on a life of their own and if for the moment they register in our minds in one particular formation, perhaps in the next moment they will morph into something completely new. This is the first layer of meaning in his work: at any moment, trying to capture any reality is akin to capturing the sea in a fish net. The center cannot hold.

Water, of course, is a favourite theme of Schneider's work, to the extent that quite often objects of dramatic solidity become liquefied when seen through his lens. Although not all objects can be dissolved in water, this does not prevent one from driving an automobile into a lake or from perceiving the lake as solid and the automobile as potentially fluid. After all, if all matter is just a matter of the Higgs Boson pushing against the fullness of empty space, why should we remain wedded to any one single interpretation of any physical manifestation? This is only one of the many questions posed by Schneider's fondness for capturing those mysterious waves that unify all material reality: we are the source of all understanding and we are passing away even as we are arriving.

In summation, Schneider's abstract images are a form of art that presents a rolling horizon of humour, perception and imagination and there is a serious scientific premise in the beauty of his distorted view of reality.

Ben Sidran, author of "There was a Fire" and creator of many music CDs.

www.bensidran.com

# Neither / Nor

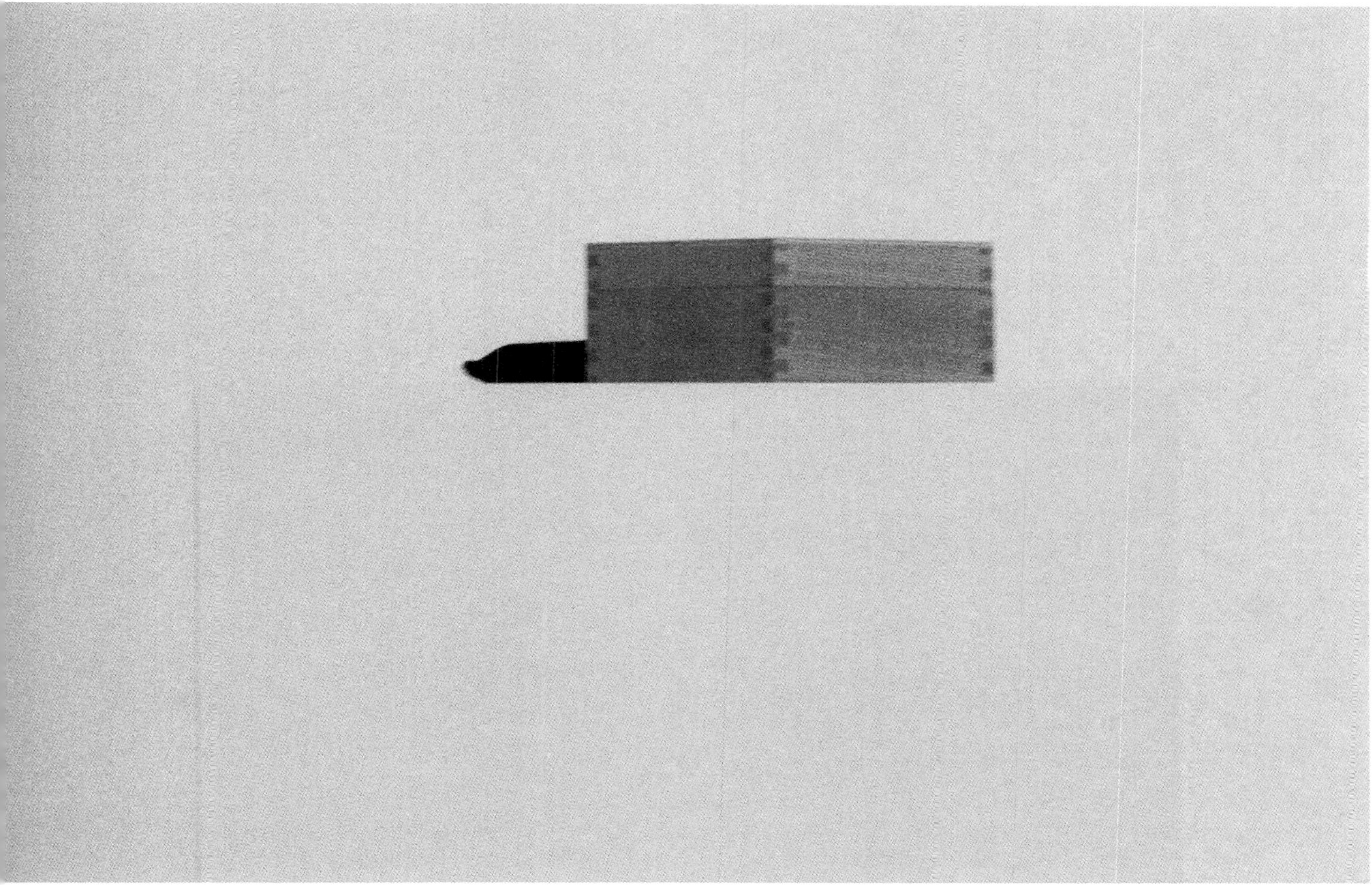

SBS
SSM

# Appendix

| | | |
|---|---|---|
| 12 | Hiddensee Island, Germany | 2013 |
| 13 | Berlin | 2014 |
| 14 | assembled in Berlin | 2009 |
| 15 | Mecklenburg, Germany | 2011 |
| 16 | Venice | 2013 |
| 17 | Berlin | 2014 |
| 18 | Venice | 2008 |
| 19 | Berlin | 2007 |
| 20 | Pierre Feu, Alp Maritim, France | 2009 |
| 21 | Berlin | 2010 |
| 22 | Venice | 2006 |
| 23 | Berlin | 1998 |
| 24 | Berlin | 2011 |
| 25 | NYC, Central Park | 1965 |
| 26 | Venice | 2008 |
| 27 | Berlin | 2007 |
| 28 | Pierre Feu | 2012 |
| 29 | Vienna | 2010 |
| 30 | Berlin | 2014 |
| 31 | Berlin | 2008 |
| 32 | Istria | 2009 |
| 33 | Arizona | 2007 |
| 34 | Berlin | 2006 |
| 35 | Berlin | 2014 |
| 36 | Berlin | 2009 |
| 37 | Pierre Feu | 2008 |
| 38 | Pierre Feu | 2006 |
| 39 | Berlin | 2013 |
| 40 | Venice | 2013 |
| 41 | Berlin | 2006 |
| 42 | The Hamptons, N.Y. | 2007 |
| 43 | Berlin | 2007 |
| 44 | Berlin | 2014 |
| 45 | Venice | 2013 |
| 46 | Arizona | 2007 |
| 47 | Istria | 2011 |
| 48 | Berlin | 1997 |
| 49 | Venice | 2013 |
| 50 | The Hamptons, N.Y. | 1978 |
| 51 | Rome | 2011 |
| 52 | Barcelona, after Gaudi Parque Güell | 1985 |
| 53 | Barcelona, after Gaudi Parque Güell | 1985 |
| 54 | Venice | 2009 |
| 55 | Venice | 2008 |
| 56 | Venice | 2009 |
| 57 | Venice | 2013 |
| 58 | Venice | 2012 |
| 59 | Venice | 2008 |
| 60 | Berlin | 2006 |
| 61 | Oxnard, CA. | 2005 |
| 62 | Venice | 2009 |
| 63 | Venice | 2013 |
| 64 | Berlin | 2006 |
| 65 | Hiddensee | 2012 |
| 66 | Pierre Feu | 2010 |

| | | |
|---|---|---|
| 67 | Pierre Feu | 2008 |
| 68 | Mecklenburg | 2011 |
| 69 | Venice | 2008 |
| 72-77 | Berlin | 2006 |
| 78-81 | Berlin | 2008 |
| 82-85 | Pierre Feu | 2007 |
| 86-87 | Berlin | 2008 |
| 88-93 | The Hamptons, N.Y. | 2007 |
| 94-99 | Madrid | 2009 |
| 100-105 | Roquesteron | 2012 |
| 106-111 | Oxnard, CA. | 2006 |
| 112-113 | Venice | 2007 |
| 116 | Yucatan | 1972 |
| 117 | Berlin | 2008 |
| 118 | Berlin | 2014 |
| 119 | Berlin | 2010 |
| 120 | Berlin | 2008 |
| 121 | Venice | 2005 |
| 122 | Berlin | 2007 |
| 123 | Sapri, Italy | 2005 |
| 124 | Venice | 2008 |
| 125 | Pierre Feu | 2010 |
| 126 | Papua New Guinea | 1977 |
| 127 | Barcelona | 1985 |
| 128 | Berlin | 2008 |
| 129 | Berlin | 2009 |
| 130 | Long Island | 1978 |
| 131 | Berlin | 2005 |
| 132 | Hiddensee | 2012 |
| 133 | Berlin | 1998 |
| 134 | India | 1977 |
| 135 | Greenwich Village, NYC | 1968 |
| 136 | Manhattan | 1973 |
| 141 | assembled in Berlin | 2010 |

This volume was assembled by
Ira Schneider with the help of Peter Wick
and scanning by Noemi Rzewski

Photographs taken from 2005 were all recorded in digital format.
A small number of earlier pictures were taken with a 16mm Bolex.

Schneider has also produced "Enjoying Depression",
a humorous e-Book for download onto iPads and Computers. It is available at the iTunes store.
For a free preview just click on the Enjoying-Depression-link on our homepage
at
www.ira-schneider.com

Please look at our website, we change it often.

Contact: ijs99@yahoo.com

print 2015

ISBN 978-3-00-048934-1